Petite Fashion
THE LONG AND SHORT OF IT

Researched and Collated by Sharron Halstead

Copyright © 2018 by Sharron Halstead
Petitepeds® is a registered trademark of Sharron Halstead
All rights reserved, including the right to reproduce this book or portions thereof in any form whatsoever. Affiliate links may be used, which is at not cost to you.

ISBN: 978-0-64519821-2-6

Credits
Cover graphics, book illustrations and Graphic Design by Karen Hue
Book creation by Luca Funari,
lucafunari@hotmail.com
Author and images: Luisa Kearney,
©OnlinePersonalStylist.com,
Sharron Halstead © PetitePeds

Contact
Email: sales@petitepeds.com.au
Website AU: www.petitepeds.com.au
Website US: www.petitepeds.co

Melbourne, Australia

Cataloguing
National Library of Australia Cataloguing-in Publication Date
Sharon Halstead's Petite Fashion, the Long and Short of It Fashion

INTRODUCTION — The Long and Short of it

Petite Fashion

I HAVE A DREAM... a dream to help Petite ladies!

Welcome

The aim of this book is to provide you with numerous tips (sourced, thoroughly researched and then compiled into one easy to read, direct and explicit beautiful book). I am confident it contains quality content to assist all you beautiful petite ladies out there who struggle with dressing your petite frames and feet.

Now in business for a few years, I have heard all the stories of woe and frustration from my petite customers, not just about shoes but clothing and fashion in general. It has been my catch cry that "Dressing a petite lady is different to dressing an average woman, period."

With a firm interest in being the authority on anything petite, I decided to invest in creating a book to dress the unique petite frame, and combined with a qualified fashion stylist so that we could assist our customers. This book is a culmination of all the research, sourced from qualified stylists, customer feedback and good old-fashioned trial and error, into this very unique E-book targeted at petite ladies. As the saying goes, "necessity is the mother of invention" so it was out of a dire need for change that this e-book was born.

targeted at petite ladies. As the saying goes, "necessity is the mother of invention" so it was out of a dire need for change that this e-book was born.

Remember this book is essentially a reference book, not to be digested in one sitting, but rather to be referred to whenever you have a fashion dilemma or want to know what goes with what, what will suit your body shape or face shape or skin colour or what accessory to match for your height etc.

I would love to get any feedback so please feel free to contact me with comments, questions or suggestions at

Yours, Fashionably

Sharron Halstead
Founder, Petitepeds

Contents

CHAPTER 1 Petite Women – what is petite? 7
CHAPTER 2 Creative through clothing 10
CHAPTER 3 Balancing out your body proportions 16
CHAPTER 4 Bra fittings (cups and sizes for petites), shapewear, underwear, swin suits 37
CHAPTER 5 Using jewellery to balance proportions 47
CHAPTER 6 Using accessories for proportions 50
CHAPTER 7 Size Guide to Petite Sizes 61
How to Mesure Your Foot 67

BIOGRAPHY 68
BONUS SECTION 69
REVIEW SECTION 70
ALSO BY SHARRON HALSTEAD 72

CHAPTER 1

Petite Woman

What is petite?

- Petite is a size determined by nothing more than height

The definition of

Petite is

adjective:
petite (of a woman) attractively small and dainty. "she was petite and vivacious"

synonyms:
small, dainty, diminutive, slight, little, tiny, elfin, delicate, small-boned;

CHAPTER 2

Creating curves through *clothing*

You have probably noticed in the media how fashion and lifestyle magazines, as well as other forms of media aimed at women are filled with articles on diets and tips for losing weight or appearing slimmer. So what if you want to create curves or appear fuller in figure?! There are more ladies out there in this position than you may think so you are not alone! Of course, you need to know just a few simple rules in order to achieve the illusion of curves in a clever and stylish way rather than looking frumpy and your dress sense misunderstood!

FASHION STYLING TIP 1:
A Peplum Hem is Your New Best Friend!

A peplum hem has "built-in" curves, as do ruffles, frills, lace, ruched garments and other textures that create volume and angles to your figure. When it comes to creating curves, you should not wear well-fitted, slim-fitting clothing, as the way to create curves is to mix varying fits and textures to create a well balanced figure. A peplum hem top for example, will give the illusion of an hourglass shaped top half, where the peplum hem at the bottom of a skirt will give the illusion of fuller hips and thighs. Ruffles on a blouse will add bulk to your bust and stomach area and ruching at the sides of tops and on the shoulders gives a more obvious waste and forms an hourglass appearance, whereas the shoulder ruching will give you more defined shoulders.

FASHION STYLING TIP 2:
Attention to Detail Best Friend!

Unlike if you wanted to appear slimmer and leaner, you do not have to worry about avoiding any loud prints or tiny detail on clothing when trying to create a fuller figure – the more the better. Big patterns, tiny detail, heavy materials and horizontal stripes are all great patterns to wear in order to look stylish and add about 10lbs instantly and to all of the right places. Note: horizontal stripes work best for adding curves; vertical stripes work best for making you look slimmer. You can also wear combat trousers and other more detailed clothing styles, which would usually add "bulk" and "volume" to many figures, but don't worry – you can afford to!

FASHION STYLING TIP 3:
Change Where You Shop Best Friend!

If you are not a teenager do not shop in teenage fashion stores. Teenage fashion clothes are designed for teenage girls and therefore give you a very child-like appearance when wearing these garments. Instead of shopping in the kids section, go to the petite section of adult fashion stores where you will find a range of "shaper" jeans, plus varying styles, fits and cuts. It may sound like hard work, but spending a little extra time looking for the right places that stock petite wear and that can cater for your needs will save you lots of cash and style frustration later on!

CHAPTER 3

Balancing Out
your body proportions

long body and short legs/ short body long legs / big chested (busty), big stomach, big arms, big butt, flat butt.

Every woman in the world has one part of her body that she feels is her "problem area." Catwalk models are considered flawless, but due to their lack of curves they often have flatter bottoms. Ladies with enviable hourglass figures often hate their upper arms...the list goes on. In some cases, no amount of exercise or strict diets will fix these problem areas, but don't worry because the next best thing is dressing to improve, fix or hide these areas!

> women are now choosing to wear hipster and low rise trousers and jeans, which is preventing them from developing accentuated waists

LONG BODY, SHORT LEGS

Fact: Longer bodies and shorter legs is a body shape that is now becoming increasingly common in this day and age! Why? Because girls and women are now choosing to wear hipster and low rise trousers and jeans, which is preventing them from developing accentuated waists. Years ago, girls from as young as 13/14 would wear waist enhancing underwear and clothing in order to develop the perfect hourglass figure where their bust and hips would be at least 9 inches wider than their waist measurement. These days not many girls or women under the age of 50 wear high waisted trousers unless they happen to be in fashion, which is why today's women have less of a difference in their waist, bust and hip measurements. This then has a domino effect on the length of their upper bodies, because regular wear of hipster jeans has lead to their bodies establishing a much lower hip line. To sum up, their hip lines will be lower meaning that their upper body will be longer – sometimes appearing almost as long as their legs.

The Fix: The best way to fix this both short-term and long-term is to start wearing higher waistbands. Wearing a waist band that reaches your bellybutton or just below will shorten the appearance of your upper body, whilst making your legs appear longer. Should you adapt this new style habit long-term, you may even be able to permanently retrain your body to establish a higher hipline and create a more obvious waist. Opt for higher waistlines on your skirts, trousers and jeans and wear shorter tops that sit above your hips.

> women are now choosing to wear hipster and low rise trousers and jeans, which is preventing them from developing accentuated waists

SHORT BODY, LONG LEGS

Fact: Typically, it is apple shaped women who suffer shorter upper bodies and longer legs. The issue that many ladies with shorter upper bodies find is that having a shorter upper body makes them appear fuller on their top half – another common issue for apple shapes. Even in petite ladies, it is possible for you to have an inside leg of 28/29" which is classed as regular in trouser sizes however, your upper body may be much shorter in comparison.

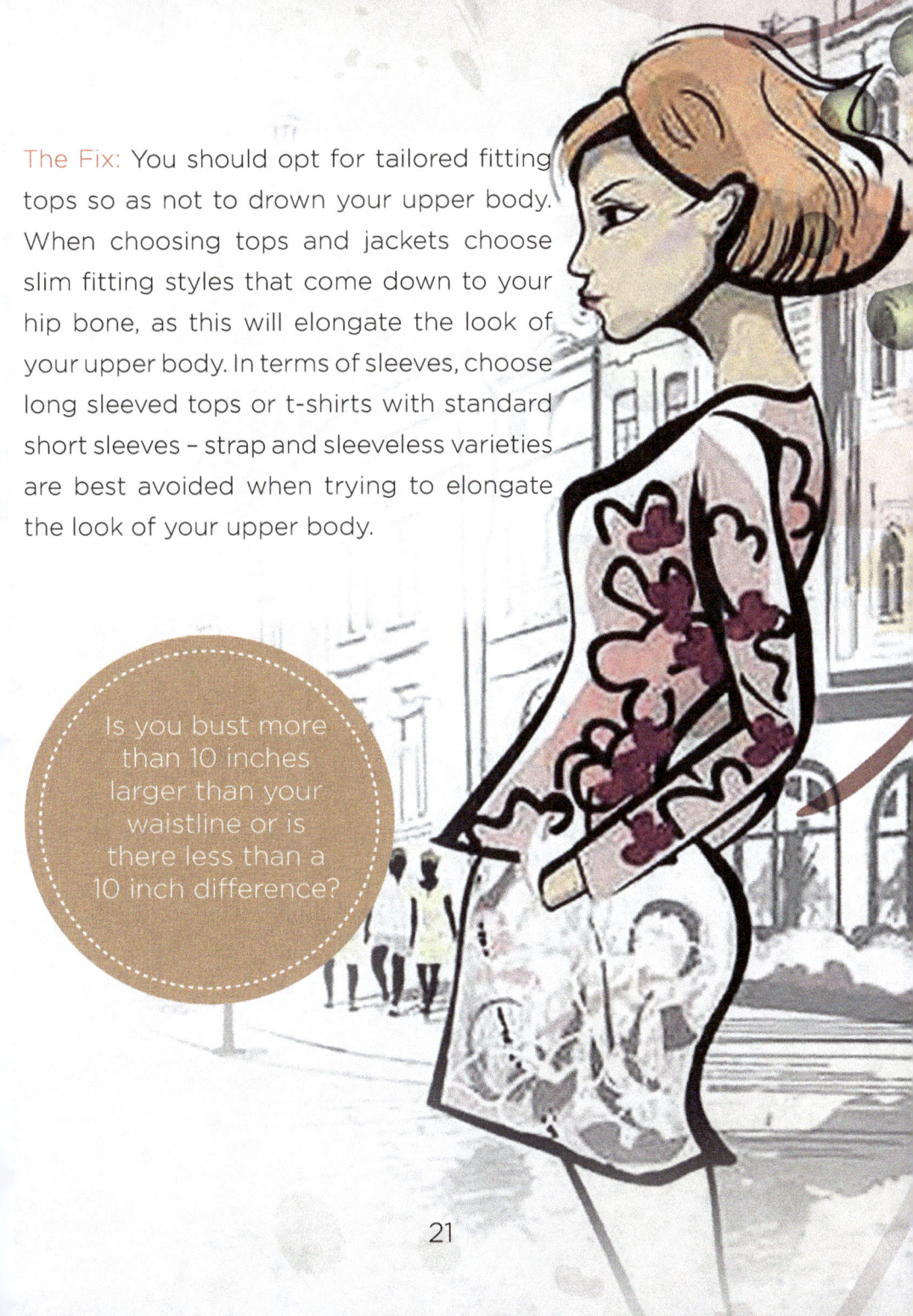

The Fix: You should opt for tailored fitting tops so as not to drown your upper body. When choosing tops and jackets choose slim fitting styles that come down to your hip bone, as this will elongate the look of your upper body. In terms of sleeves, choose long sleeved tops or t-shirts with standard short sleeves – strap and sleeveless varieties are best avoided when trying to elongate the look of your upper body.

Is you bust more than 10 inches larger than your waistline or is there less than a 10 inch difference?

Big Chest / Big Bust

Fact: When trying to disguise or dress down a larger bust, you need to be perfectly clear on whether your bust is more than 10 inches larger than your waistline or is there less than a 10 inch difference? If there is less than a 10 inch difference then you're more likely to be apple shaped and should consult the advice below on dressing down a larger waistline and upper body. If your bust is 10 or more inches bigger than your waistline then your bust indeed will be one of your fullest measurements, in which case you need to read on.

Avoid short tops and jackets that sit above your hip bone.

As you have probably found out, having a fuller bust has as many advantages as it does disadvantages. Although many of your friends may envy your curves, dressing for day to day life can prove challenging. In the right dress or outfit, accentuating a larger bust can appear very sophisticated and feminine however, in your daily life you may want to make your bust appear a little less obvious or simply make it appear in proportion with the rest of your body. In some cases, a fuller bust can make you look up to a couple of sizes larger than you actually are as well, which is why it is useful to know how to balance out your fuller bust.

See below for examples:

The Fix: It can seem tempting and appropriate to wear a baggy top or tunic to completely disguise your bust. This may help you to feel more elegant and slimmer. Unfortunately this is the wrong thing to do! Not only does wearing a baggy, oversized top or tunic make your bust appear the same size or fuller, it also makes the rest of your body covered by the top appear the same size as your widest measurement – which is most likely going to be your bust. You may be surprised to learn that the best way to disguise or reduce a larger bust is to wear fitting upper body garments that come down to your hip bone and also – take note of the neckline which is very important! A narrow neckline will make your bust appear fuller, which is why you should avoid round necks. V-necks are good if you want to accentuate an hourglass figure, but if you want to balance out a fuller chest, opt for wider neck lines, such as:

- Square necks
- Wide round necks
- Wide v-neck tops

Avoid tops that are very baggy around your waist area

WIDER WAISTLINE

Fact: Wider waistlines usually belong to those who have very slim hips. Quite often ladies who have very petite bone structure with narrow shoulders and hips often have wider waistlines. Don't be confused by this – although ladies in this category are prone to carrying extra weight around their waistlines, this doesn't always have to be the case, you may just have a less accentuated waist that's not many inches smaller than your hips. Either way, the same rules on dressing a wider waistline still apply.

Avoid short tops and jackets that sit above your hip bone.

To Fix:

- Stop wearing clothing that doesn't do you any favours. One of the most common habits of all people with less accentuated waistlines is that they choose to wear garments that were made for ladies with different body shapes to theirs.
- You need to choose longer tops and upper body garments which must come down to your hip bone (no higher).
- Avoid short tops and jackets that sit above your hip bone.
- Avoid wearing patterned tops and jackets. Instead stick to plainer colours or if you like wearing patterns, wear patterns on your bottom half and plainer colours on your top half.

- As you do not have a narrow waistline, do not wear clingy belts that sit on your waist. If you have a tiny waist line then these look great but if not, they will only add fullness to your waistline which is not what you want.
- Wear v-neck tops.
- Avoid tops that are very baggy around your waist area.
- If you have slimmer shoulders and arms, choose tops and jackets with well fitting arms and with more detail around the shoulder area, this will give the illusion of (only slightly) slightly fuller shoulders and a narrower waistline.

WIDER UPPER ARMS

Fact: Your wider upper arms may be down to you carrying more weight on your upper body or down to the fact that you workout a lot, both of which can result in wider upper arms.

The Fix: You can fix this issue easily through jewellery or sleeves!

- Bigger watches and bracelets will make the tops of your arms appear smaller.
- Wear longer sleeves.
- When wearing t-shirts, find longer sleeves that are slightly longer than standard t-shirt sleeves but not as long as sleeves.
- When wearing longer sleeves, try to find tops that have buttons at the wrists or that are turned up at the wrist or that have some other detail at the wrist. This will take the emphasis off of your upper arms and help to slim and elongate them.
- Avoid strap tops.
- Avoid tube tops.
- Avoid sleeveless tops.

When layering your tops, try to wear the same colour but different shades, rather than two or more different colours completely, which will create an extreme contrast and could make your arms appear shorter and wider.

- Avoid strap tops.
- Avoid tube tops.
- Avoid sleeveless tops.
- When layering your tops, try to wear the same colour but different sha es, rather than two or more different colours completely, which will create an extreme contrast and could make your arms appear shorter and wider.

A Bra can make you look slimmer, curvier, taller, shorter, so getting it paramount to your fashion success

WIDER BOTTOM

Fact: Some trousers and bottoms will make your bottom appear wider – even if you do not actually have a wide bottom. Wider bottoms usually mean that your body shape type is pear shape. This means that you have slim arms, a slim top half, small waist but fuller hips, butt and thighs. The mistake than many ladies who fall into this category make is that they create too much of a contrast between their upper and lower body, thus making their upper body appear very narrow and their lower body appear very wide. This is usually because they mix up the patterns and styles that they should actually be wearing in the opposite places, i.e. certain prints are best for their upper bodies, other styles are best for their lower bodies.

The Fix: Combat trousers are many women's "go to" style staple when they have larger thighs, hips and bottoms but this is one of the biggest mistakes you can make and will only make your thighs and butt appear wider even though combats may seem like a sensible option. The buttons and detail on the outer sides of most combat trousers draw attention to these areas and make your lower body appear fuller. Many ladies in this category hate jeans because they fear that jeans will highlight their fuller lower body when in fact, some jeans can actually be a savior!

- Avoid patterned trousers, stick to plainer colours and styles
- Avoid lots of detail on bottoms – i.e. lots of buttons, pockets, zips, etc.
- Keep your bottoms plain and opt for more interesting patterns on top to balance out the difference between your upper and lower body.
- When choosing jeans opt for darker colours or with lighter jeans such as stonewash and white choose a size up or a looser fitting style.
- When choosing jeans, try to find a pair that are dark on the outside of the leg and lighter in the middle. This is like "contouring for legs" – it will shrink the width of your bottom and legs.

- Be mindful when choosing back pockets on trousers.

- If you want to slim down your derrière then opt for larger back pockets and these will make this area look smaller. On the other hand, if you are trying to fake a larger bottom then go for smaller back pockets.

- Avoid thick materials or boxy materials. Choose softer, more moveable fabrics to help prevent further contrast in your body shape.
- Avoid sleeveless tops.

- When layering your tops, try to wear the same colour but different shades, rather than two or more different colours completely, which will create an extreme contrast and could make your arms appear shorter and wider.

FLAT BOTTOM

Fact: Besides from hourglass figures, every type of body shape can have a flat bottom even of you have fuller legs and wider hips. Although having a flat bottom can be frustrating at times when you try on trousers and jeans in stores and find that you're unable to fill them out like you wanted to, having a smaller bottom means that you can always "add to it." With the help of a little pattern, some well places pockets, stripes, buttons and detail you can easily fake a rounder, pert, and fuller bottom without having to do a single squat!

The Fix: Basically, you need to do everything and wear everything that somebody from the pear shape category shouldn't!

- Back pockets that are close together give the illusion of a toned curved bottom, whereas pockets that are spaced apart will give the illusion of a fuller bottom.

- Wear bottoms with detail around the upper thigh and bottom area.

- Try to choose bottoms with a thick waist band instead of a small, standard waistband. The thicker waistband will accentuate a bottom of any size.

Bigger watches and bracelets will make the tops of your arms appear smaller.
- Wear longer sleeves.
- When wearing t-shirts, find longer sleeves that are slightly longer than standard t-shirt sleeves but not as long as sleeves.
- When wearing longer sleeves, try to find tops that have buttons at the wrists or that are turned up at the wrist or that have some other detail at the wrist. This will take the emphasis off of your upper arms and help to slim and elongate them.
- Avoid strap tops.
- Avoid tube tops.
- Avoid sleeveless tops.

When layering your tops, try to wear the same colour but different shades, rather than two or more different colours completely, which will create an extreme contrast and could make your arms appear shorter and wider.

CHAPTER 4

Bra fitttings

(cups and sizes for petites)
shapewear, underwear, swim suits

Underwear is a loved or loathed kind of topic. Underwear can play such an important role in the way our outfits can appear. One of the most important items of underwear is bras. Bras can change your shape, your appearance, they can make you look slimmer, curvier, taller, shorter... so getting to grips with understanding which bras are for you is very important. Unless you love buying underwear, buying a bra is perhaps a chore to you or something you know you have to do but not something you want to spend too long over when choosing.

Even if you don't want to spend lots of time browsing over which bra to buy, you should go into a store equipped with the basics so that you will instantly know and understand which bra is best for you. There are so many different types of bras to choose from these days so it is only understandable that it can get rather confusing but this is why you need to know the effect that each bra has on your body and appearance. Depending on whether or not you have had children, whether you have a bigger cup size or a wider under bust measurement, the right bra for you will be different to the bras that others may wear.

> If you are petite and have a small frame then wearing a band size that is too large and has straps that are very thick may overpower your delicate frame and narrow shoulders

Have you ever wondered why some bras that were made especially for your (small/normal/large) bust do not look as good as they should? That's because you have to consider the shape of your bust as well as the size.

Generally, there are 4 different types of bras for 4 different bust shapes and sizes.

These are:
- Small bust size
- Normal bust size
- Large bust size
- Lack of breast substance

The latter – lack of breast substance is where many women go wrong when buying bras. Even if you have a large bust, if you lack substance in the upper front part of your breast then some bras for big-busted ladies will not look as flattering as they could.

So what is breast substance?

Breast substance is the tissue in the top part of your breast; it is the part below your collar bone and is where the breast starts – it is also the "cleavage" part that may sometimes be shown when wearing a low cut top. Instead of choosing large open cups, choose bras with a thick band a lot of support underneath the cups which will help make the top half of your bust appear fuller and more shapely.

Another important point to remember when choosing underwear is the importance of getting measured properly. If you are petite and have a small frame then wearing a band size that is too large and has straps that are very thick may overpower your delicate frame and narrow shoulders.

Bras for Fuller Busts.

So, if you have a larger, fuller bust you will need a lot of support but nothing too bulky as that will drown your frame.

- So, if you have a larger, fuller bust you will need a lot of support but nothing too bulky as that will drown your frame.

- Choose bras with a thick band a lot of support underneath the cups which will help make the top half of your bust appear fuller and more shapely.

HERE ARE SOME OPTIONS FOR FULLER BUSTS

BRAS FOR SMALLER BUSTS

BRAS FOR BUSTS WITH LESS BREAST SUBSTANCE

If you are petite and have a small frame then wearing a band size that is too large and has straps that are very thick may overpower your delicate frame and narrow shoulders.

Shapewear

Let's not also forget the use of shapewear! Shapewear has become increasingly popular over recent years due to the fact that it is affordable and can easily reduce the look of your body weight and shrink your shape by inches and pounds in an instant! Shapewear is a type of underwear that can be worn under your normal garments. Shapewear "pulls you in" like how an old fashioned corset would do but minus the pain, complicated application and discomfort. There are various types of shapewear available, some include:

- Shapewear for leggings
- Shapewear for your bust
- Shapewear for your stomach
- Upper body shapewear - tightening the appearance of all of your upper body
- Lower body shapewear - tightening the appearance of all of your lower body r wider/fuller.

Mastering the perfect underwear is great, but what about swimwear? Usually, whenever you come to wear swimwear you are most likely to be in public, which is why you want to look your best. In order to look your best in swimwear (no matter your size or age), you need to find the right kind of swimwear for your shape.

If you have a small bust or lack substance in the upper part of your breasts then here are some excellent suggestions on the right kind of (flattering) swimwear for you. As you will see, some of these show more detail around the chest and neck area, which will add the illusion of fullness to your upper body and bust area, giving you a more balanced figure.

If you have a larger or fuller bust then these swimsuits and bikinis would be better for you, as they will suit your body shape more, emphasizing your curves but without looking distasteful or too revealing.

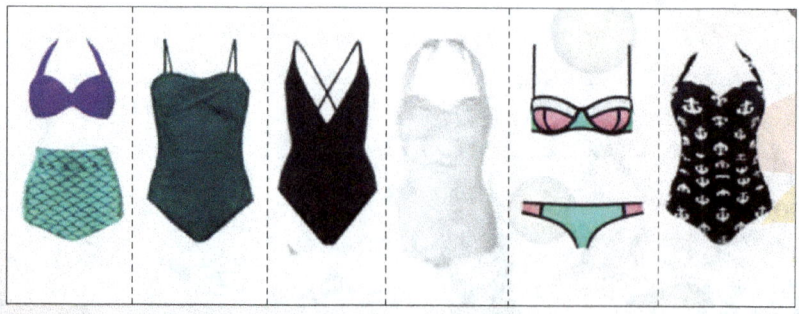

CHAPTER 5

Using jewellery

to balance your body proportions

TOP TIPS:

- Large bracelets and watches slim down and elongate your fingers, wrists, hands, forearms, upper arms and waist area.
- Small bracelets and watches add fullness to your fingers, wrists, hands, forearms, upper arms and waist area.
- Small rings slim down and elongate your fingers, wrists, hands, forearms, upper arms and waist area.
- Large rings add fullness to your fingers, wrists, hands, forearms, upper arms and waist area.
- Long earrings, single-colour earrings, earrings that sit against your face slim down your face, chin and neck.

- Wide, rounder, small, detailed, colourful earrings make your face, chin and neck appear fuller, shorter and rounder.
- Thick chain/decorative, costume jewellery-type short length necklaces shorten your neck but make the top half of your body appear smaller.
- Thin, long chains elongate your neck but neither slim or increase the size of your body.
- Thin, short chains shorten the length of your neck and make your upper body appear wider/fuller.

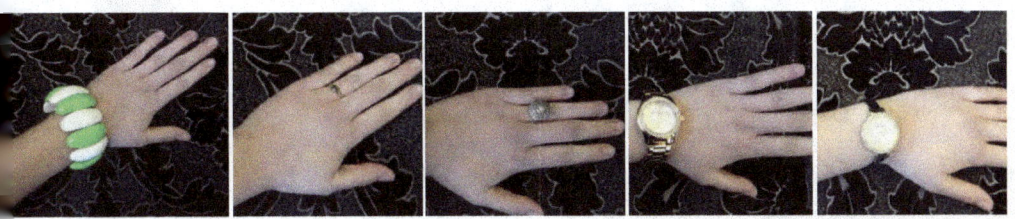

CHAPTER 6

Using other *accessories* to dress

There are so many items that you need to consider when getting dressed for the day. As well as finding the right clothing to fit your shape, you also need to find the right accessories that will suit you as well.

During the year, other items such as hats, scarves, glasses and handbags prove as very important for practical reasons and to polish off a desired look.

Finding accessories to suit your size and height is actually one of the most enjoyable and easiest parts of dressing.

As a petite lady because you can go into almost any store and find something that will suit you perfectly. Quite often, ladies who fall into the category of petite tend to go wild buying accessories on a shopping trip but are more likely to be unsuccessful when buying clothing or footwear! (That is until Petitepeds arrived!! www.petitepeds.com.au)

However there are few things that can go wrong when shopping for accessories. But with a few points to consider to steer you in the right direction, accessory shopping will be a breeze!

Hats

Don't be afraid of hats! Hats are extremely practical in the very hot and very cool weather. Having a bad hair day? It's hats to the rescue! In a rush and don't have time to do your hair? Throw on a hat and instantly look cool and stylish in seconds – nobody will ever know that you're hiding messy hair underneath! The right hat can add height to your frame, whereas the wrong hat can make you appear shorter. Some hats can look extremely flattering, whereas others can drown a narrow frame.

Don't be afraid of hats! Hats are extremely practical in the very hot and very cool weather. Having a bad hair day? It's hats to the rescue! In a rush and don't have time to do your hair? Throw on a hat and instantly look cool and stylish in seconds – nobody will ever know that you're hiding messy hair underneath! The right hat can add height to your frame, whereas the wrong hat can make you appear shorter. Some hats can look extremely flattering, whereas others can drown a narrow frame.

When choosing hats you want to avoid:

- Huge, oversized hats.
- Hats with bows on them.
- Hats with ribbons that hang in front of your face.
- Cowboy style hats with an under the chin tie

Hats to consider include:

- Round hats that are not too wide
- Baseball caps
- Small hats
- Bobble hats with a bobble on top (the bobble will add height to your body)
- Trilby hats

Scarves

Scarves are an accessory that can keep you warm in the winter, as well as make an outfit look smarter or more casual in the right situation. You will see that there are often various styles of scarves available, from those that are very short and used as wrist scarves, silk scarves used for fashion purposes, shawls, snoods and thick winter scarves. Different types of scarves suit di ferent people. For e.g. short scarves rarely suit tall people, whereas long, oversized scarves look too overpowering for anybody who is apple shaped or under 5 ft 5. You will see many fashion models wearing very long, oversized scarves which may be up to 2 metres long in length and 30cm wide, but these can be very difficult to wear if you are not 5 ft 9 with a straight type of body shape. Wearing a scarf that is too long will cover the majority of your body, on the other hand tying it and folding it will add bulk around your neck and chest area, which will again make you look several inches shorter, as well as out of proportion.

Scarf Definitions:

- Thick winter scarf: long scarves worn in the winter, varying in length (some are short and others are very long and can span the entire length of your body).
- Snood: a round scarf that sits comfortably around your neck. These can come in woollen varieties or softer, lighter varieties and depending on the material used they can be worn all year round. Snoods do not have two end pieces like a typical scarf, they are round and can be simply put round your neck and doubled up if too long – they make putting on a scarf quick and easy.
- Shawl: shawls (see below) are used as a cover up on the beach and can also be worn with formal wear, such as with a dress. Shawls are an excellent alternative to light jackets and cardigans..

Here are some scarves that will suit you perfectly. Note how they are not as long, but how it is still quite possible to find an excellent range of stylish and attractive scarves for all purposes and seasons.

- Scarves with pointed ends such as the first picture below will give the illusion of a slimmer, taller figure.
- Also, experiment with different ways of tying your scarf, as some people find it more comfortable to wear their scarf in certain styles which perhaps suit them better.

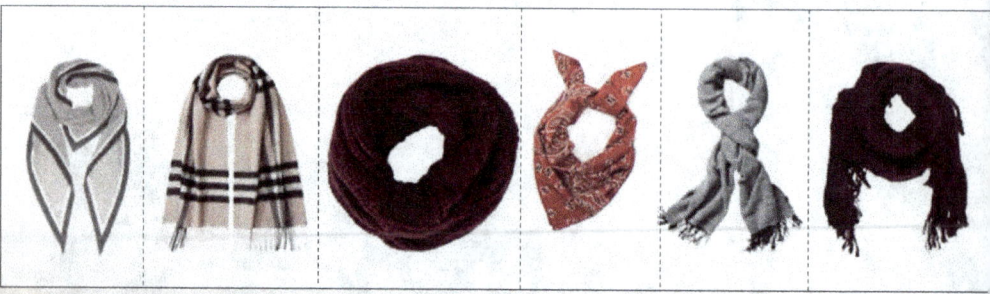

Glasses

The type of glasses and sunglasses that will suit you will depend on your face shape and personal preferences. The most important point to remember when choosing glasses is not the style and shape but the width of the glasses. The most common problem that affects petite ladies more than anybody else when shopping for glasses is that they often end up buying "on-trend" styles which are actually too big for their smaller bone structure. This issue affects petite ladies of all weights and body shape, no matter your face shape or any other contributing factor. Many curvier ladies at 5 ft 2 who have round face shapes suffer this problem too because they buy and wear sunglasses that are too wide for their face and forehead. To avoid this problem, make sure that when testing out glasses (sunglasses or normal glasses) that the sunglasses do not come away from your face – they should not exceed the width of your head.

- The best shape sunglasses for petite ladies are those with smaller frames. Wayfarer sunglasses and smaller aviator sunglasses are an excellent option, as well as round sunglasses and cat eye sunglasses with smaller frames and lenses. Here below are some excellent options for you that won't overpower or hide all of your face.
- Top tip: If you have stronger, more defined bone structure then choose softer frames. If you have less defined bone structure then choose thicker, heavier frames.

> The best shape sunglasses for petite ladies are those with smaller frames.

Handbags

The good news about finding handbags that will compliment your height and shape is that you can wear any size handbag and it will look great!

The bad news is that you need to pay attention to the shape!

Wide, oversized handbags that appear "floppy" and untailored are not ideal for ladies under 5ft3. Wide handbags in general are best avoided because they can easily add fullness to the point of your body at which they sit, such as under your shoulder, at your waist, at your hips or near your thighs. Large, oversized handbags that resemble the style of beach bags can also make you appear far shorter than you really are, because these kinds of bags can actually make you look as though you are carrying luggage rather than a handbag.

Handbags

What you want to look for are bags that are longer in length rather than wide and try to choose bags that look more tailored in design, rather than bags that have no obvious shape.

Longer straps are an excellent idea too, as these will elongate your upper body and legs. Remember that you can wear both small and large bags, just make sure that when choosing larger handbags that you choose handbags that are longer, more tailored in appearance and that have a prominent shape to them.

Here are some fantastic styles to choose from:

CHAPTER 7

Size Guide to
Petite sizes

International Clothing Size Guide

Petite = 5 ft 3 and under

Euro size	Australia size	UK size	Length (CM)	Circumference (CM)
35	1	2	233.31	234.5
36	2	3	239.98	239.0
37	3	4	246.65	243.5
38	4	5	253.32	248.0

UK Sizes (inches)	XS (6)	S (8-10)	M (12-14)	L (16-18)	XL (20-22)	XXL (24-26)
Bust	33"	34-35"	36-37"	$38^{1/2}$-40"	$41^{1/2}$-$43^{1/2}$"	$45^{1/2}$-$47^{1/2}$"
Waist	25"	26-27"	28-29"	$30^{1/2}$-32"	$33^{1/2}$-$35^{1/2}$"	$37^{1/2}$-$39^{1/2}$"
Hips	35"	36-37"	38-39"	$40^{1/2}$-42"	$43^{1/2}$-$45^{1/2}$"	$47^{1/2}$-$49^{1/2}$"
Arm length (petite)	29"	$29^{1/4}$ - $29^{1/2}$"	$29^{3/4}$ – 30"	$30^{1/4}$-$30^{1/2}$"	$30^{3/4}$-$30^{7/8}$"	$33^{7/8}$-34"

International Bra Sizes & Guide

A common issue among ladies with small bone structure is that they require a small band size in their bra but need a larger cup size. For e.g. you may try a bra that's a UK size 34A but find that the band is too large for the size of your back but the cup fits fine. In this case you need to go down a band size and up a cup size – this is a handy trick to know if you do not have the opportunity to go for a professional bra fitting or in the case that a bra you've tried doesn't fit the same way that others in that size do.

Here below is the full list of "petite bra sizes" and their international size equivalents.

AUSTRALIA / NZ	USA	UK / INDIA	EUROPA / CHINA / JAPAN / HONG KONG / KOREA	FRANCE / SPAIN / BELGIUM
8AA	30AA	30A	65A	80A
8A	30A	30B	65B	80B
8B	30B	30C	65C	80C
8C	30C	30D	65D	80D
8D	30D	30DD	65E	80E
8DD	30DD	30E	65F	80F
10AA	32AA	32A	70A	85A
10A	32A	32B	70B	85B
10B	32B	32C	70C	85C
10C	32C	32D	70D	85D
10D	32D	32DD	70E	85E
10DD	32DD	32E	70F	85F

AUSTRALIA/NZ	USA	UK/INDIA	EUROPA/CHINA/JAPAN/HONG KONG/KOREA	FRANCE/SPAIN/BELGIUM
14F	36F	36G	80H	95H
14G	36G	36H	80I	95I

AUSTRALIA/NZ	USA	UK/INDIA	EUROPA/CHINA/JAPAN/HONG KONG/KOREA	FRANCE/SPAIN/BELGIUM
10E	32DDD/F	32F	70G	85G
10F	32F	32G	70H	85H
10G	32G	32H	70I	85I
12AA	34AA	34A	75A	90A
12A	34A	34B	75B	90B
12B	34B	34C	75C	90C
12C	34C	34D	75D	90D
12D	34D	34DD	75E	90E
12DD	34DD	34E	75F	90F
12E	34DDD/E	34F	75G	90G
12F	34F	34G	75H	90H
12G	34G	34H	75I	90I
14A	36A	36B	80B	95B

Measuring Shaft & Heel Height

A Ankle boots
Boot shaft height is
2"-8"(Approx. 5.08cm-20.32cm)

B Mid-calf boots
Boot shaft height is
8"-14"(Approx. 20.32cm-35.56cm)

C Knee-high boots
Boot shaft height is
14"-20"(Approx. 35.56cm-50.8cm)

D Over Knee-high boots
Boot shaft height is
20" or Taller (Approx. 50.8cm or Taller)

A Flat
Shoe heel height is under
1"(Approx. < 2.54cm)

B Low Heel
Shoe heel height is
1"- 1
3/4" (Approx. 2.54cm-5.08cm)

C Mid Heel
Shoe heel height is
2"-2
3/4" (Approx. 5.08cm-7.62cm)

D High heel
Shoe heel height is
3"-3
3/4" (Approx. 7.62cm-10.15cm)

E Ultra High heel
Shoe heel height is
4" or Taller
(Approx. > 10.15cm)

Shoe Size Conversion Chart

A combination of Foot Length, Width and Arch comprises a person's exact shoe size. Example if 2 people have the same foot length but their width and arch is different they WILL wear different size shoes.

Australia	US	Europe	UK	Asia	China	Foot Length (cm)	Foot Width (Girth) cm	Foot Arch (cm)
1	2	32	13	210	32	18-20	20	21
2	3	33	1	215	33	19-20	21	21
2.5	4	34	1.5	220	34	19-20	22	23
3	4.5	34.5	2	225	34.5	21.5		
3.5	5	35	2.5	230	35	22.8		
4	5.5	36	3	235	36	23.1		
4.5	6	37	3.5	240	37	23.5		

How to find your size

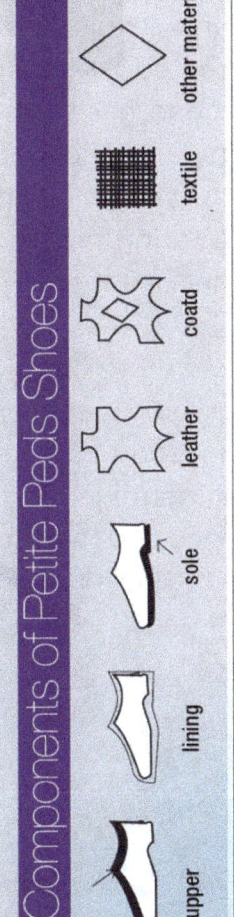

Foot Girth
- Measure in bare foot
- Measure the widest part of each foot

Foot Length
- Measure in bare foot
- Straight-line from bottom line to top

Foot Arch
Measure in Barefoot
Measure around the arch of the foot

Components of Petite Peds Shoes

| upper | lining | sole | leather | coatd | textile | other material |

www.petitepeds.com

Biography

Sharron Halstead is the Founder of Petitepeds, a global online shoe store catering exclusively to ladies with petite feet.

After receiving a multitude of enquiries, comments, complaints, expletives from customers who were fed-up of being treated like second class citizens by the fashion houses, Sharron and her team went about writing "Petite Fashion – The Long and Short of It" to help petite ladies find their own style and sass, and not be at the mercy of a fashion retail world catering primarily to the average size body and foot, but rather use their unique advantage to get the best out of it.

From humble beginnings out of her garage in Melbourne, Australia, she has spread her wings into global markets to assist all petite ladies, the world over, find themselves, their confidence and their self esteem by learning about the basics on how to dress their unique body shapes and petite feet.

Dear Petite Lady,

As a thank you for purchasing this book, I'd like to give you a FREE E-Book specifically written to help you on your journey in transforming your Personal Style and Image.

Please visit
http://bit.ly/petitepeds
to claim your FREE Copy TODAY!

Dear Petite Lady,

hope you enjoyed reading this book as much as I enjoyed putting it together for you. As you can see it is not a book that you read once, but more of a reference library for all things Style for the Petite Lady.

If you enjoyed the book and found it useful, I'd be very grateful if you would post an honest review on our Amazon Page as well as on our Google and Facebook Page.

Your support really does matter and will make a difference, not only to us but also to the countless Petite ladies who want to purchase the book.

I do read all the reviews so I can get your feedback in real time.
Here are the links to leave reviews:

Here are the links to leave reviews:

Facebook Review   http://bit.ly/PetitepedsFB

Google Review   http://bit.ly/PetitepedsGoogle

Amazon Review   http://bit.ly/PetiteFashion1

Thank you for your Support!

Sharron

Founder, PetitePeds

www.ingramcontent.com/pod-product-compliance
Lightning Source LLC
Chambersburg PA
CBHW071841290426
44109CB00017B/1892